EXCAVATING THE PAST

THE AZTEC EMPIRE

Dr Nicholas Saunders and Tony Allan

Heinemann Library
Chicago, Illinois

© 2005 Heinemann Library
a division of Reed Elsevier Inc.
Chicago, Illinois

Customer Service 888-454-2279
Visit our website at www.heinemannlibrary.com

Designed by Carole Binding
Originated by Ambassador Litho Ltd
Printed in China by WKT Company Limited

09 08 07 06 05
10 9 8 7 6 5 4 3 2 1

**Library of Congress Cataloging-
in-Publication Data**

Allan, Tony, 1946-, Saunders, Nicholas, 1953-
  The Aztec empire / Tony Allan,
  Nicholas Saunders
      v. cm. -- (Excavating the past)
  Includes bibliographical references and index.
  Contents: A world lost and found --
Rediscovering the Aztecs -- Growing up Aztec --
How the Aztecs rose to power -- Life in the Aztec
capital -- Lords and slaves -- Shrines and sacrifices
-- Warfare and warriors -- The end of the Aztec
world.
  ISBN 1-4034-4839-6 (lib. bdg.) -- ISBN 1-4034-
5459-0 (pbk.)
  1. Aztecs--History--Juvenile literature. 2. Aztecs--
Social life and customs--Juvenile literature. 3.
Aztecs--Antiquities--Juvenile literature. [1. Aztecs.
2. Indians of Mexico.] I. Title. II. Series.
  F1219.73.A46 2004
  972'.00497452--dc22
                            2003023731

Acknowledgments
The author and publisher are grateful to
the following for permission to reproduce
photographs:

pp. 5 top and bottom, 6 top and bottom, 7 top,
bottom, 10 top and bottom, 11 top and bottom,
12 top, 13 top, 14 top, 15 top and bottom, 17
bottom, 18 bottom, 19 right, 20 center, 21 top,
right, and bottom, 22 left, 23 top and bottom,
24 left and bottom, 25 center, 27 bottom right,
28–29 center, 29 top right, 31 center, 32 left, 34,
35, 36 top and bottom, 37 top right, 38 top and
bottom, 39 right, 40–41 center, 41 right and
bottom, 43 center Art Archive; pp. 8–9 top, 16
top, 19 left and bottom, 25 top right, 26 bottom,
33 left and right, 37 bottom right, 42 center
Werner Forman Archive; p. 12 center Ancient Art
and Architecture; pp. 26 top, 27 top Dr. Michael
Smith; p. 43 top Alamy.

Cover photograph of the Pyramid of the Sun
reproduced with permission of Corbis. The small
photograph of the feathered shield reproduced
with permission of Werner Forman Archive.

Some words are shown in bold, **like this.** You
can find out what they mean by looking in
the glossary.

CONTENTS

A WORLD LOST AND FOUND

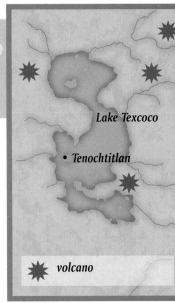

For more than 3,000 years the volcanic highlands and tropical rain forests of Mexico have been home to many civilizations, including the Olmecs, the Toltecs, and the Maya. The most famous culture is probably that of the Aztecs. The Aztec empire grew, flourished, and died in less than 200 years. It was the last of ancient Mexico's great civilizations, destroyed at its height by Spanish invaders led by Hernán Cortés. By C.E. 1519, the Aztec empire covered more than 77,220 square miles (200,000 square kilometers) of land and was home to at least three million people, who spoke over twenty different languages.

The Aztec homeland

The Aztecs arrived in the Valley of Mexico around C.E. 1300 after moving south from their homeland in northern Mexico. The Valley of Mexico was a rich and fertile place, dominated by Lake Texcoco, and surrounded by an active volcanic landscape. This geography and the sophisticated civilization of nearby ruined cities such as Teotihuacan inspired Aztec civilization and **mythology**. They called the area *Anáhuac* (land by the water's edge), and used the word *altepetl* (mountain of water) to describe any village or town.

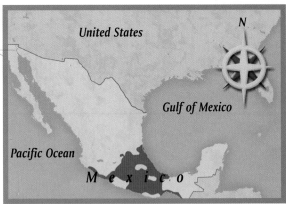

▲ The map above shows the extent of the Aztec empire in red, and its position in modern-day Mexico. The top map shows the area around the Aztec capital, Tenochtitlan. Lake Texcoco is shown as it exists today.

A civilization destroyed

In 1519, Spanish soldiers known as **conquistadors** arrived in Mexico in search of treasure. The Spaniards, with their guns and metal armor, were much better armed than the Aztecs, who fought with spears and bows and arrows. By 1521, Hernán Cortés had

> ▷ The Aztecs had no weapons to match the Spanish soldiers, known as conquistadors. The Spaniards had guns, but the Aztecs had only spears, clubs, and bows and arrows.

conquered the Aztecs and claimed their empire and the whole of Mexico for Spain. No complete or undamaged Aztec monuments have survived because the Spanish destroyed the city during the **siege** of 1521. The Spaniards looted and destroyed the Aztec capital of Tenochtitlan, and then built their new city, Mexico City, over the ruins. The speed of this rebuilding meant there was no time to destroy temple foundations or the many large stone **sculptures**. They were simply covered with rubble and built upon, preserved for future generations of archaeologists to discover.

The rediscovery of the Aztecs

The new rulers had no interest in the **pagan** Aztec heritage, which went against their **Christian** culture. They tried to hide or destroy its remains. From the 1700s, however, interest in Aztec culture began to develop. Scholars created collections of Aztec **artifacts**, old manuscripts were discovered and published, and new monuments were unearthed in Mexico City. Throughout the 1800s and 1900s, more monuments and temples were uncovered and great advances were made in understanding Aztec art and **glyphs**.

WHO WAS Hernán Cortés?

Hernán Cortés (1485–1547) was a Spanish soldier who, as a young man, went to seek his fortune on the Caribbean island of Hispaniola. The governor of the island put him in charge of an expedition to explore the Mexican mainland. As soon as Cortés saw the gold and other riches in Tenochtitlan he decided to conquer it. After his victory in 1521, he became governor of New Spain (Mexico). Later he set up several other, unsuccessful expeditions to explore unknown parts of North America. He finally returned to Spain in 1540, where he died seven years later.

DID YOU KNOW? The Aztecs copied architecture from past cultures such as the Toltecs.

The birth of Aztec archaeology

First excavations

The earliest large **excavations** took place in the 1790s in the *Zocalo*, the main square of Mexico City. Many of the most famous monuments were found in these early excavations, including the Coatlicue statue and the Stone of the Sun. During the 1800s, further discoveries were made by chance when foundations needed to be dug for new buildings. The discoveries included a sculpture of the goddess Coyolxauhqui, unearthed in 1825.

△ *This is the excavation site of the Great Temple in Mexico City. Excavations lasted from 1978 to 1982, and many exciting objects were found, including a gruesome **skull rack**.*

Into the 20th century

The first planned excavation in Mexico took place in 1913 after workers demolishing a building uncovered the southwest corner of the Great Temple in Mexico City. Further excavations continued around the temple's base through the 1960s. During the 1970s, **archaeology** in Mexico City became more organized. Several excavations began in areas of Tenochtitlan. Then, a lucky find by workers digging a pit for power supplies led to the discovery of the Coyolxauhqui Stone at the base of the Great Temple. The site was thought to be so important that in 1978, the President of Mexico issued an order authorizing its excavation. Since then, so many discoveries have been made there that the Museum of the Great Temple was opened in 1987 to display them.

△ *This gold pendant shows Mictlantecuhtle, the lord of the dead, who was believed to rule the hells beneath the earth. It was found at the Great Temple site in Mexico City.*

▷ *This is the Mesoamerican Gallery in the National Museum of Anthropology in Mexico City. The museum houses such major finds as the Stone of the Sun and the Stone of Tizoc. Treasures from other ancient Mexican cultures are also here.*

WHO WAS William H. Prescott?

William H. Prescott (1796–1859), a historian from the United States, was the man who did most to inform people about the Aztecs. He finished writing his book, titled History of the Conquest of Mexico, *in 1843. As exciting as an adventure story, the book was an instant success. People still read it today to learn about the Aztecs and the Spanish soldiers who conquered them.*

The quest goes on

Since the Aztec civilization lasted for such a short period (about 200 years), it did not leave many monuments. In addition, many of the great temples and palaces the Aztecs built were destroyed by the Spanish conquerors. Archaeologists investigating the Aztecs concentrate on smaller sites, excavating houses to find out how ordinary people lived. These excavations have produced many everyday objects such as knives made of a dark glass called obsidian, bronze sewing needles, and stone mortars for grinding maize.

Archaeology Challenge

The Aztec writing system used several kinds of **glyphs.** Pictograms showed an object by its picture. Ideograms expressed an idea, such as footprints to mean travel. Other signs were used where the sound of one word was similar to the sound of a different word, and could be used to express it. To read or write Aztec glyphs and make connections between sounds required a lot of knowledge and practice.

LISTENING TO THE AZTECS

One of the most valuable sources available to historians and archaeologists studying the Aztecs are the accounts written by their Spanish conquerors. There are also accounts called **chronicles**, written by **monks** who traveled from Spain to teach Christianity to the Aztecs. Finally, there are texts called **codices** by the Aztecs and their neighbors of the time, which help us to imagine what life would have been like in the Aztec empire.

Accounts from the front line

Spanish **conquistador** and chronicler, Bernal Díaz del Castillo, had served in the **New World** under various commanders before joining Hernán Cortés in 1519 to help conquer Mexico. His huge work, *The True History of the Conquest of New Spain*, was written when he was an old man living in Guatemala in Central America. It tells of Díaz's experiences as a soldier serving Cortés, and describes life as a common soldier and the people he met in Mexico.

During his time in Spain, Hernán Cortés wrote five letters to the King of Spain. They provide a first-person account of the conquest of Mexico. The letters also describe his problems with creating a government, trying to get recognition for his achievements from the King and Queen of Spain, and struggling to keep his power and influence. Cortés's later letters became bitter and arrogant as eventually he lost all his power.

△ *This is a painting of friar Bernardino de Sahagún. His writings about the Aztecs were unread for hundreds of years, because the authorities wanted to suppress all knowledge of the Aztecs.*

△ *Aztec codices had no covers, but were protected by a wooden board at each end.*

Aztec books and famous friars

Bernardino de Sahagún (1500–1590) was a Spanish monk who worked in Mexico as a **Christian missionary.** He persuaded some surviving Aztecs to help produce a book of picture writing, a codex titled *The General History of the Things of New Spain* (often known as the *Codex Florentine).* Friar Diego Durán spent his childhood in Mexico and learned much about Aztec culture. His *Book of the Gods and Rites* and *Historia de la Nueva España* provide the most complete account of the people of the region.

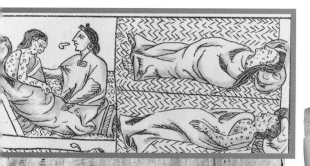

Codex Florentine

This codex was compiled by Bernardino de Sahagún in the late 1500s. He spoke with old men and had them draw in the traditional way. The book has information on daily life, **rituals,** health, and myths. The illustration above shows an Aztec woman suffering from smallpox, a disease brought to Mexico by a Spanish slave.

Archaeology Challenge

There are many different kinds of codices, each dealing in its own particular way with various aspects of life in ancient Mexico. They seem to offer straightforward accounts of religion, everyday life, and the Spanish conquest, but in reality they are not easy to understand. Each codex has its own problems of **bias** in terms of who made it, when, and why. Finding hidden meanings, allowing for Spanish **prejudices** and Aztec ideas of history, as well as the problem of translating *Nahuatl* into Spanish, means each codex must be carefully analyzed if it is to be used accurately.

A wealth of information

The codices

The Aztecs and their **ancestors** "wrote" about their history, religion, and daily life using a picture-based language called **pictographs**. Scribes or priests drew the pictographs in books called **codices**. The Spaniards burned most of the codices because they viewed them as against Christianity, but some have survived. Most codices contain paintings of religious ceremonies, gods, and kings, rather than everyday life, although the Codex Mendoza is an exception.

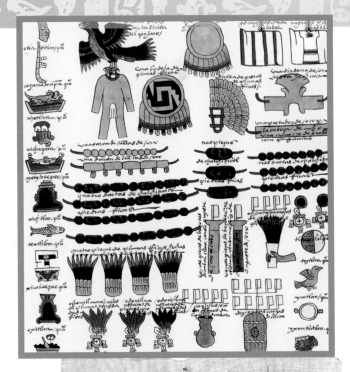

Key codices

No true Aztec codex has survived from pre-Spanish times. What we have today are codices produced by neighbors of the Aztecs, such as the **Mixtecs**. Others were painted by Aztecs after the conquest under the direction of Spanish priests like Bernardino de Sahagún. Most codices contain pictures with Spanish captions, though some are mainly written accounts. During the early years of Spanish rule, local communities produced documents in a native style called *lienzos*. They often included maps of their villages and were used in their dealings with the Spanish.

Codex Mendoza

The Codex Mendoza is a collection of Aztec pictures revealing Aztec customs and history. It was painted soon after the Spanish conquest, on the order of the first Viceroy of New Spain (Mexico) to be sent to the King of Spain, Charles V. To help the king understand it, a Spanish priest who had learned the Aztec language wrote explanations in Spanish by each picture. This page from the Codex Mendoza shows the tribute (tax) to be paid by a particular city to Tenochtitlan. It includes clothing, jewelry, and a warrior's equipment.

Fragile evidence

The case of the Codex Borgia illustrates how easily codices could be damaged over time. Also known as the Book of Prophecies, Cardinal Stefano Borgia, a collector of **pagan** and Christian **artifacts**, found it in the hands of children, who had set it on fire. Unfortunately, the Cardinal was not able to rescue the first and last pages of the codex. On his deathbed in 1804, he gave it to the Catholic church. Today, the Codex Borgia is held in the Vatican Library in Rome, Italy.

Codex Magliabecchiano

The Codex Magliabecchiano was illustrated for scholar Dr. Cervantes de Salazar around 1553. It has sections on the ancient calendar, monthly feasts, and other festivals. The page above shows the "Pulque Feast," with women serving maguey root beer. The Codex Magliabecchiano has fine drawings, along with a short Spanish commentary. It is one of the main sources in understanding the Aztec's monthly festivals.

Codex Borbonicus

The Codex Borbonicus was made in Tenochtitlan, probably soon after the conquest, and contains spaces meant for comments by the Spanish. It tells the reader about how the Aztec world was created, and about the Aztec gods. This page shows the god Xipe Totec and his feathered serpent Quetzalcoatl, surrounded by **glyphs** of Aztec calendar symbols.

The Codex also shows the important "New Fire Ceremony" that occurred every 52 years.

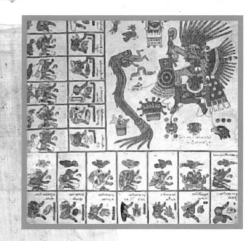

The Aztec capital of Tenochtitlan lies today beneath the streets of modern Mexico City. Whenever building work takes place, traces of the Aztec city re-emerge. Temples, painted platforms, and statues of gods have all been discovered in recent years. During the early 1960s, the pyramid-temple at Tlatelolco with its twin stairways was **excavated**, and in 1967 archaeologists discovered and restored a circular temple to Quetzalcoatl.

△ *This illustration shows the building of Tenochtitlan, from the* Historia de los Indios *by Diego Durán.*

Founding Tenochtitlan

The first page of the Codex Mendoza shows an eagle perched on a cactus growing from a stone. The codex describes how this had been

△ *An artist's reconstruction of part of Tenochtitlan shows the Great Temple in the center*

foreseen in a vision by the Aztec god Huitzilopochtli as the place where the Aztec city should be built. The Aztecs named it Tenochtitlan. The Codex Mendoza's opening page also shows the four quarters into which the city was divided. By measuring the positions of buildings and examining 16th-century Spanish maps, archaeologists have shown that Tenochtitlan was built on a grid plan aligned to the gods' position in the sky. The east-west line was considered the most important because it tracked the path of the sun god Tonatiuh each day. Excavations beneath the cathedral during the 1970s revealed the remains of the Temple of the Sun God, the circular Temple to Quetzalcoatl, and the foundations of the great **skull rack** *(tzompantli)*.

EYEWITNESS

"Proud of itself is the city of Tenochtitlan. This is your glory, O Giver of Life."

15th century Aztec poem

A city of canals

The city's layout included roads and a system of canals that linked all parts of the capital. The first page of the Codex Mendoza shows four blue crossed bands, representing the canal system.

△ *This is a modern painting of Tenochtitlan from the Museo Ciudad Mexico.*

Canoe transport was common, and the Spanish commented on how crowded the surrounding lake was. Knowledge of water control enabled the Aztecs to build dams, keeping fresh and salty water separate. Part of a giant **aqueduct** built to bring drinking water from the mainland has been reconstructed in the center of Mexico City.

Archaeology Challenge

Somewhere beneath the streets of downtown Mexico City lies one, possibly two, great **ball courts** of Tenochtitlan. A plan of the Great Temple in the Florentine Codex shows shows the "L"-shaped structure near the skull rack, but archaeologists have not yet located it. According to the Codex Magliabecchiano, the ball game, *tlachtli,* is played with two players representing each of the two teams, a rubber ball, and two hoops set high on the side walls.

Written evidence

There are a number of descriptions of Tenochtitlan set down by Cortés himself in his letters to the King of Spain. In the second letter he describes his first encounter with the city of Tenochtitlan: "After half a mile we arrived at the great city of Tenochtitlan which is situated at its center. We met with three cities all containing very fine buildings and towers, especially the houses of the chief men and the . . . little temples in which they keep their idols."

City life

Tenochtitlan was a huge city, home to a dazzling array of craftspeople, artisans, traders, and priests, as well as the Aztec royal family and their servants. The city was an **imperial** capital in whose markets and storehouses could be found every kind of plant, animal, and mineral from across Mexico and beyond. The Codex Mendoza illustrates the wealth of items demanded as tribute (tax) from

△ *This 20th-century painting by Mexican artist Diego Rivera of the busy market in Tenochtitlan is based on descriptions by Spanish soldiers.*

the 450 cities ruled by the Aztecs. These items included different kinds of cloth, animals and skins, birds (and their feathers), tortoise shells, **jade**, and reed mats, as well as maize, honey, amber, and gold. Trade was what kept Tenochtitlan alive. It took place in marketplaces across the capital, but was dominated by the huge market at Tlatelolco.

City living

Spanish **chronicles** include detailed descriptions of the Aztec capital and reveal their astonishment about what they saw there. At the heart of the city was the great ceremonial square with the Great Temple and other important buildings. Ordinary people lived in white, flat-roofed houses a single story high; it was a crime for anyone but nobles to have two stories or more. Wealthy citizens lived in bigger houses hidden behind windowless walls. Inside, the rooms opened out onto a central courtyard, often with a pond and gardens of brightly colored flowers.

Tlatelolco market

Everyday about 25,000 people thronged the marketplace, and every fifth day a special market attracted 50,000 people. Spaniards who saw the market were amazed at its size and the quantity and variety of its goods. **Conquistador** Bernal Díaz del Castillo describes walking among sellers of cacao beans, goldsmiths, and dealers in tobacco, tree-bark paper, salt, and slaves. The market even had its own group of judges who maintained fair play in business transactions.

Craftspeople

Tenochtitlan had a wide variety of craftspeople. Feather-working was a special skill, used to make cloaks and costumes for warriors and nobles. Montezuma II owned a famous headdress made from shimmering green feathers, which he gave to Hernán Cortés as a gift in C.E. 1519. Stonemasons carved statues of the gods, metalsmiths made gold jewelry, and other workers produced sharp blades for tools and sacrifices, as well as brightly polished mirrors.

Cacao beans for money

In 1536, a Spanish priest named Father Motolinía wrote that cacao beans (cacahuatl) served as money as well as being the main source of chocolate. Spanish conquistadors observed how an obsidian blade cost 5 cacao beans, a turkey 100 cacao beans, and a jade necklace 60,000 cacao beans. Like all **currencies,** cacao bean money could be copied illegally. In the 1550s, a Spanish official named Oviedo noted that cacao shells were emptied and re-filled with soil.

DID YOU KNOW? The Aztecs called craftspeople *tolteca*, in honor of the Toltec civilization. **15**

RELIGION AND SACRIFICE

In 1978, workers in downtown Mexico City accidentally dug up a great stone disk carved with the image of the Aztec Moon goddess Coyolxauhqui. It had been placed at the foot of one of the staircases of the Great Temple. Archaeologists then **excavated** below the square and found the *tzompantli,* or **skull rack**, outside the Great Temple. In total, archaeologists spent five years excavating the remains of seven temples. They discovered 78 buildings and an array of incredible finds, including statues and offerings to the gods.

△ *The Coyolxauhqui Stone was found at the Great Temple site in 1978. It shows the body of Coyolxauhqui, the moon goddess, and sister of the god Huitzilopochtli.*

The Great Temple

The Great Temple was a stepped pyramid, called a *teocalli* (god house) in the **codices**. Work began on it in C.E. 1325, and the temple was built in line with two sacred volcanoes nearby. On its **summit** were **shrines** to the rain god Tlaloc and the war god Huitzilopochtli. It was here that human sacrifices took place, acting out the events shown in the codices. The Great Temple contained the most important group of religious buildings in the Aztec capital of Tenochtitlan. The Spanish regarded the frightening images of gods and the bloody sacrifices that honored them as devil worship. Beginning in C.E. 1525, they forced the Aztecs to destroy the temple. There was no time to remove the lower sections of the Great Temple. This meant that the remaining sections were built over and accidentally preserved for almost 500 years.

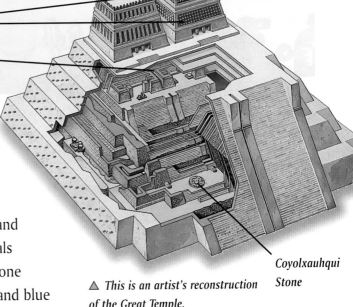

shrines to Tlaloc and Huitzilopochtli

sacrificial altar

Coyolxauhqui Stone

△ This is an artist's reconstruction of the Great Temple.

Burials and offerings

At the Great Temple, archaeologists found 100 burials full of offerings to the gods. Some offerings contained human remains such as skulls decorated with shell and turquoise pierced by **flint** knives. Many burials contained beautifully painted pottery and stone **sculptures** dedicated to Tlaloc. Their green and blue colors were meant to reflect the god's mastery of rain, water, and fertility. The *tzompantli,* showing 240 human skulls carved in stone, was one of the most gruesome discoveries. The top of the altar probably once held the heads of sacrificial victims. Animal sacrifice was also important in Aztec society. Other finds included complete skeletons of jaguars with green **jade** balls in their fangs, pumas, or crocodiles surrounded by seashells and jade.

EYEWITNESS

"There are, in all districts of this great city, many temples or houses for their idols. They are all very beautiful buildings. . . . Among these temples there is one, the principal one, whose great size and magnificence no human tongue can describe . . ."

Letter written by Hernán Cortés, the Spanish military leader

△ The tzompantli, *or skull rack, at the Great Temple in Mexico City.*

The Aztec gods

The Aztec world was alive with powerful gods and the spirits of the **ancestors**. Paintings of them adorned the walls of the Great Temple, and filled the pages of the **codices**. Aztec gods represented different aspects of life. One example is Xipe Totec, god of springtime, who wore the skin of a victim sacrificed in his honor. As the skin dried and fell away, the Aztecs believed it encouraged the newborn corn cob to burst forth from its crinkled leaves. However, Xipe Totec also had the power to send people diseases if they offended him. Other gods and goddesses included Chicomecoatl and Xilonen, who were often shown wearing corn cobs. They represented growth and fertility.

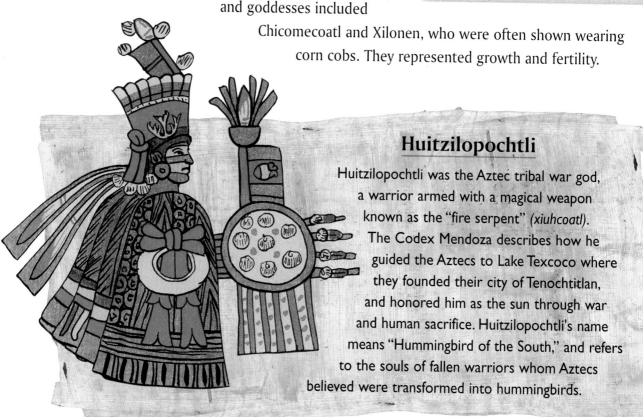

Huitzilopochtli

Huitzilopochtli was the Aztec tribal war god, a warrior armed with a magical weapon known as the "fire serpent" (*xiuhcoatl*). The Codex Mendoza describes how he guided the Aztecs to Lake Texcoco where they founded their city of Tenochtitlan, and honored him as the sun through war and human sacrifice. Huitzilopochtli's name means "Hummingbird of the South," and refers to the souls of fallen warriors whom Aztecs believed were transformed into hummingbirds.

Gods of the elements

There were also gods that represented the powerful forces of nature. They appeared as supernatural characters in the codices, shaping the world through epic battles, and giving life to every feature of the earth and heavens. There were gods of wind, fire, and water, of childbirth, disease, and misfortune, as well as of the sun, moon, and stars. There were two special gods in Aztec religion—the sun god Huitzilopochtli, and the rain god Tlaloc. Each was worshipped in his own **shrine** on the **summit** of the Great Temple.

Coyolxauhqui

The Aztecs believed Coyolxauhqui, goddess of the Moon or the Milky Way, was the evil sister of Huitzilopochtli. When she discovered her brother was about to be born she murdered her mother Coatlicue. She failed to prevent the birth, and in revenge, Huitzilopochtli killed her and **dismembered** her body at the sacred hill of Coatepec. This horrible scene was carved on a huge stone disk at the base of the Great Temple.

Tezcatlipoca and Quetzalcoatl

Tezcatlipoca was the most powerful Aztec god. Master of sorcery and human sacrifice, he saw everything through his magic mirror. He inspired such fear that the Aztecs described themselves as his slaves. Quetzalcoatl, the "Feathered Serpent," was a kind god of learning, twins, and inventor of the calendar. He often appears disguised as Ehecatl, the wind god.

Tlaloc

Tlaloc represented water and fertility. Together with his assistants, the *tlaloques,* he sent the rains and made the crops and flowers grow. His paradise of Tlalocan shimmered with sunlight, jewels, and rich vegetation, and was the final resting place of the disabled, those killed by lightning, and those who had drowned.

"All the walls of the shrine were so splashed and caked with blood that they and the floor too were black. The whole place stank horribly."

Spanish soldier Bernal Díaz del Castillo, describing the shrine on top of the Great Temple of Tenochtitlan, where sacrifices were carried out

Sacrifice

Sacrifice lay at the heart of Aztec religion and society. The act of sacrifice, whether human or animal, was seen as the continual repayment of the debt humans owed to the gods. Pyramid-temples and **shrines** at which gods were worshipped through acts of **ritual** death were found across the capital.

Aztec priests

Spanish priests recorded the activities of their Aztec counterparts in order to understand, then destroy, Aztec religion. They described Aztec priests as the guardians of sacrificial bloodletting rituals. Every night they pierced their bodies, then pulled reeds through the holes. Spanish priests also commented on the smelly and blood-soaked clothes these priests wore.

Self-sacrifice and victims

The gods Quetzalcoatl and Tezcatlipoca are shown in art and **mythology** piercing their bodies to draw blood. **Codices** and **sculptures** show people piercing every part of their body, though usually the tongue, ears, legs, and arms, collecting the blood in a dish and then burning it. Human sacrifices were the ultimate and most valuable acts of worship. So important were they that victims were regarded not as unworthy humans, but rather as "god impersonators." They were groomed for their eventual death in order to please the gods.

▲ This statue of Coatlicue shows the goddess dressed in a skirt of writhing snakes, with huge animal claws for hands and feet, and a necklace of severed hands and hearts and a human skull.

◁ *This beautiful turquoise mask had a sinister purpose. It was used in sacrificial ceremonies, and the person who wore it was probably killed and eaten.*

Sacrificial tools

Knives were used to cut out human hearts and **dismember** bodies. These have been found in many places in downtown Mexico City. Black volcanic glass was used, and was identified with the god Tezcatlipoca, the inventor of human sacrifice. **Stingray** spines were also used, as were maguey cactus thorns. The former have been found in the Great Temple.

▷ *This flint knife was probably used in sacrificial ceremonies to cut out the heart of a victim.*

Heart sacrifice

The pyramid at Santa Cecilia, and the innermost part of the Great Temple, had hot coals next to their shrines where human hearts were burned. Heart sacrifice was regarded as repeating the myth in which Huitzilopochtli killed his sister, the moon goddess Coyolxauhqui. The ritual is shown in the Codex Magliabecchiano, with priests carrying victims to the temple **summit**, stretching them over the sacrifice stone, and cutting out their hearts.

Archaeology Challenge

It took experts almost 100 years to work out that the statue found in 1790 represented Coatlicue. They did so by comparing it with other known pictures of the goddess and noting that it shared certain common features—especially the serpent skirt. Today much more is known about the Aztec gods, making the job of identifying them easier.

△ *The temple at Santa Cecilia is one of the best preserved Aztec buildings.*

AZTEC SOCIETY

In 1845, a plaque named the Dedication Stone was found in Mexico City. On it were the names of the emperor Ahuitzotl, his predecessor Tizoc, and the date 1487. It was made to celebrate a major renovation of the Great Temple. The date is important because from this point on, Aztec society quickly became an **imperial** civilization, with Ahuitzotl conquering 45 new towns according to the **Codex** Mendoza. The vast wealth in taxes that flowed into Tenochtitlan transformed Aztec society; public **rituals** became more elaborate and human sacrifices increased in number.

△ *In the gardens at the center of Montezuma II's palace, the emperor had his own private zoo, with pumas, jaguars, birds of prey, and rattlesnakes.*

The sacred emperor

The Dedication Stone helps archaeologists understand how a person became emperor. The plaque shows the two emperors Ahuitzotl and Tizoc sacrificing their blood to the earth to mark Ahuitzotl's succession. The dedication of the newly refurbished Great Temple was the final ceremony in his becoming emperor.

The Florentine Codex tells archaeologists about the power an emperor had in Aztec society. It shows rulers seated on thrones covered with the skins of powerful animals such as the jaguar. This codex also records that during the coronation of emperors they prayed to their patron god Tezcatlipoca for guidance, and identified themselves with him. Spanish priest Bernardino de Sahagún also records the final ceremony of the coronation involving a period of seclusion and blood offerings.

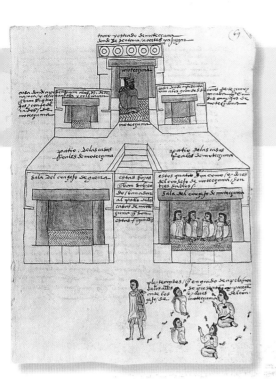

◁ *This **pictograph** from the Codex Mendoza shows Montezuma's palace. The emperor is at the top, in the throne room. Below are meeting rooms for his generals and advisors.*

Royal palaces

Royal palaces were like small towns, with thousands of servants, courtyards, jails, and storerooms. King Nezahualcoyotl of Texcoco had a summer palace at Texcotzinco where he created a terraced garden with birdcages and waterfalls, all fed by an **aqueduct**. Today, the remains form an important archaeological site, where the ritual baths, rooms, and rock carvings are still visible.

Facts from the Florentine Codex

Each new emperor underwent a series of colorful rituals before beginning his reign. Dramatically staged events included the coronation itself, the new emperor fighting a Coronation War to prove his military abilities, and a final confirmation ceremony. The Florentine Codex describes the emperor making speeches to Tezcatlipoca, the patron god of royalty. The emperor asks for strength and guidance in his many sacred duties. Once crowned, he was carried on the jaguar-and-eagle throne to the Great Temple where he pierced his body with a jaguar claw in a blood offering that tied him forever to the gods.

WHO WAS Montezuma II?

*Montezuma II ruled between C.E. 1502 and 1520, and was emperor at the time of the Spanish conquest. Unlike the earlier Montezuma I, Montezuma II added little territory or tribute (taxes) to the empire, concentrating instead on holding on to previous gains. His indecisiveness when faced with Hernán Cortés and the **conquistadors** led to his being captured and imprisoned, then killed by his own people for working with the Spanish.*

Nobles, commoners, merchants, and slaves

Aztec society was based on class. The top ten percent were nobles, though inheritance was less important than achieving high status through one's own actions. Several key figures helped the emperor rule the empire, and they are shown in the **Codex** Mendoza, seated in the Council Hall that was part of Montezuma II's palace. The most important office was Snake Woman (Cihuacoatl). Despite the name, the position was occupied by a man.

Nobles

The Codex Mendoza shows Aztec nobles wearing their distinctive cloaks, and seated on reed thrones. Nobles paid no taxes, and were provided with an official residence from whose agricultural lands they drew their livelihood. The sons of Aztec lords were born into a junior class of nobles known as the *pipiltin,* from which the emperor selected many of his high officials.

△ *This image from the Codex Mendoza shows a nobleman wearing a colored cotton cloak.*

The merchants

Merchants known as **pochteca** belonged to a special class in Aztec society. A *pochteca* trading expedition was sometimes the first step toward war. It was also dangerous, and the gruesome death of *pochteca* merchants is shown in the Codex Mendoza. This stone model, found in the Great Temple, shows a *pochteca* carrying goods using a headstrap.

▷ *This is a **jade** model of an Aztec* macehualtin *of the peasant class. By law, they were not allowed to wear fine clothes.*

Commoners

Most Aztecs were commoners, or **macehualtin,** though they could become nobles if they acted with distinction. They were organized into hereditary clans known as *calpulli* which themselves were divided into units of 20 families and arranged in groups of 100 households. Each *calpulli* had its own school and temple, and was controlled by a leader elected for life. The benefits of belonging to a *calpulli* were not shared by the free, but landless peasants known as **mayeques.** They were either not Aztec, or had lost their rights through crime or debt.

△ *This **pictograph** from the Codex Vaticanus shows Chalchiuhtlicue, goddess of lakes and rivers, being attended by slaves. In Aztec society, slaves were often given as tribute by conquered tribes.*

The slaves

No one was born into slavery, and slaves, or **tlacotin,** formed perhaps only two percent of the Aztec population. Although their work was unpaid, they enjoyed free food and shelter, did not pay taxes, and did not serve in the army. *The Book of the Gods and Rites* has a market scene that shows traders buying and selling slaves who have large wooden collars around their necks to prevent escape. Despite this image, slaves could achieve high status, own land, and even acquire slaves of their own.

DID YOU KNOW? When nobles visited the emperor, they had to dress in plain clothes.

25

Farming, food, and country life

Most evidence about Aztec life comes from the **codices** and archaeological **excavations** at the Great Temple in Mexico City. These provide information on religious **rituals** in the capital, its temples, and the life of the upper classes, but they tell us little about ordinary people in the countryside. Recent excavations at the small villages of Capilco and Cuexcomate, and the larger rural city of Yautepec, provide an exciting insight into life in the Aztec countryside.

△ *Families at Cuexcomate and Capilco lived in small, one-room houses with sun-dried mud brick walls and thatched roofs. The foundations of this house can still be seen.*

Country life

The small farming village of Capilco had 21 houses, while Cuexcomate had 150. In late Aztec times, it appears that the population was growing since excavations have uncovered evidence for an increase in dam-building to water more land and produce more food. Locals were not poor. Obsidian, bronze tools, and expensive beautifully-made painted pottery have been found in almost every house. Finds of paper nearby suggest families seem to have been making bark-tree paper in their spare time, too.

The Floating Gardens

The Floating Gardens of Mexico City are the remains of a system of agriculture known as the *chinampas*. The Aztecs adopted this ancient system at Tenochtitlan, producing fertile garden plots by dredging the lake floor to create artificial islands separated by canals. Kept in place by willow trees, the rich soil that developed was used to grow flowers, chilies, tomatoes, maize, and many other plants.

A "rural" city

Seven Aztec houses were excavated at the Aztec city of Yautepec. They were only a little larger than those at Cuexcomate. Arts and crafts, however, were more developed. Plentiful evidence indicates that the population included workers making blades and tools, potters making clay figurines, and other specialists involved in making cotton textiles, and also jewelry. An unexpected discovery was the royal palace of Yautepec's king, which became the first Aztec palace ever to be excavated. Its courtyards, rooms, and passageways were originally covered with bright paintings.

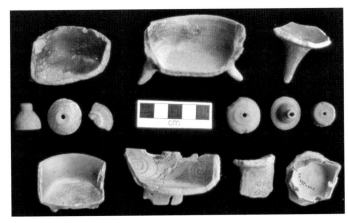

△ *Broken pieces of ceramic cooking pots, storage jars, serving bowls, and tortilla griddles give evidence for the preparation of meals by the women of Capilco and Cuexcomate.*

Food and drink

The codices tell us that Mexico was particularly rich in vegetable foods. There were no horses or cattle, so all agriculture was done by hand. The staple food was corn cobs, ground into flour and baked as **tortillas,** or steamed as tamales stuffed with vegetables, meat, and sometimes frogs. Tomatoes, chilies, rabbit, deer, and turkeys were eaten, as was a hairless breed of dog. Insect eggs and water fly larvae were delicacies, and chocolate was drunk by the higher classes. The main drink was the alcoholic *pulque* made from the maguey cactus.

▷ *This picture from the Codex Vaticanus shows farmers harvesting maize. This was the main food in the Aztec diet.*

DID YOU KNOW? The emperor Montezuma finished every day with a cup of chocolate.

AZTEC TIME

In 1790, long after the Aztec civilization had been destroyed by the Spanish conquest, workers laying drains in Mexico City's main square came upon a round stone covered in mysterious carvings. It measured 4 feet (1.2 meters) thick, 10 feet (3 meters) across, and weighed 26.5 tons (24 metric tons). The workers reported their find to the authorities, who recognized it as an **artifact** from Aztec times. Today this relic, known as the Stone of the Sun, is seen as one of the most important finds in Tenochtitlan and is exhibited in Mexico's National Museum. Together with the **Codex** Borbonicus, it casts light on the Aztec world and their view of time.

The Stone of the Sun

The Stone of the Sun is a large circular stone slab covered with intricate and once brightly-painted carvings. These designs were originally thought to represent the Aztec calendar but are now recognized as showing the five periods (or "suns") of creation in Aztec **mythology**. The Stone of the Sun is a giant **sculpture** showing the history of the Aztec universe. The detail of the carving shows that the Aztecs were extremely skilled craftspeople.

The Codex Borbonicus

The records of the 260-day religious calendar, or *tonalpohualli,* were kept by priests in sacred books known as *tonalamatl.* One of the most famous examples is the Codex Borbonicus, whose pages were divided up to show brilliantly colored paintings of the thirteen Lords of the day and nine Lords of the night. These were arranged to show their power over individual hours and days, and also over important thirteen-day weeks. The *tonalamatl* were magic books used by priests to predict future events and luck or misfortune in an individual's life.

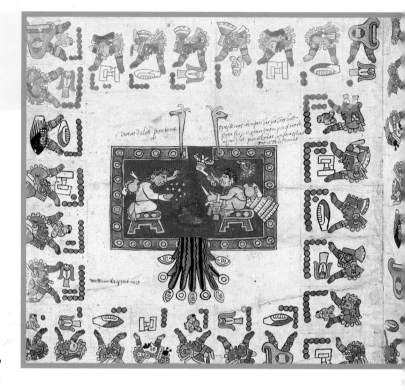

△ This illustration, from the Codex Borbonicus, shows the invention of the Aztec calendar.

The two-calendar system

The Aztecs inherited a two-calendar system from earlier Mexican civilizations. The everyday calendar, or *xiuhpohualli,* had 365 days, and was divided into 18 months of 20 days each; the extra five days were regarded as particularly unlucky. The smaller religious calendar, or *tonalpohualli,* had 260 days, and was divided into 13 months of 20 days each. The two calendars fit together like cog-wheels, and produced a different date every day for 52 years before starting again. This is called the "calendar round." At the beginning of every new 52-year period, the Aztecs celebrated the New Fire ceremony, which saw the lighting of fires across the empire as a sign of renewal.

The Stone of the Sun in detail

The Stone of the Sun's designs tell us how the Aztecs viewed time. It shows the four worlds that have ended, and the creation of the current fifth world, thought to have been created by the Aztec gods. Aztec priests were responsible for organizing the fifth world's time into hours, days, weeks, months, and the 52-year calendar round. In the religious calendar, or *tonalpohualli*, Aztec "weeks" lasted 13 days, with each week controlled by such gods as Tlaloc or Quetzalcoatl. Each of the 20 days of a month was identified with a god, also shown on the Stone of the Sun. Those named after the rabbit *(tochtli)* were ruled by Mayahuel, goddess of the maguey drink. Those born on rabbit days were doomed to live a miserable drunken life. For those born under the jaguar sign a glorious future as a warrior awaited them. The illustration on page 31 shows how the Stone of the Sun would have once looked.

Fantasy or Fact?

*The Stone of the Sun contains a **glyph** called 13-Reed, which marks the date of creation of the fifth world era by the Aztec gods. This new era or "sun" was a renewal of the world, and thus started the clock running for the sacred cycles of 52-year periods known as the calendar round. Each new 52-year period was celebrated by the New Fire ceremony. Its timing was calculated by **astronomers** who watched the movements of the group of stars known as the Pleiades. As they passed overhead, the sun rose, and a fire was sparked in the chest of a sacrificial victim. Warriors lit torches in the fire and carried them to Tenochtitlan to rekindle the temple fires. The world had been saved for another 52 years.*

Day and Year Glyphs

lizard	serpent	eagle	motion
wind	rabbit	water	dog
monkey	grass	reed	ocelot
vulture	first knife	flower	death
rain	crocodile	deer	house

▽ *This reconstruction of the Stone of the Sun is from the National Anthropological Museum in Mexico.*

The signs outside the center represent the twenty named days contained in one month. They are also used for naming years.

In the center of the Stone is the face of the Sun God Tonatiuh, with a sacrificial flint knife for a tongue and a claw on each side. This central part of the Stone represents the fifth and current period of creation.

The Sun God is surrounded by four boxes, each containing the date of the destruction of the previous four worlds. Carved in Aztec glyphs, these earlier periods were 4-Jaguar (destroyed by jaguars); 4-Wind (destroyed by hurricanes); 4-Rain (destroyed by fire); and 4-Water (destroyed by floods).

The outer rim shows two fire serpents meeting face to face at the lower extreme. They are considered to represent the creation of the fifth world.

Archaeology Challenge

The Stone of the Sun's images and glyphs were once thought to be a combination of sundial and calendar, used to calculate the dates for religious festivals. Advances in understanding Aztec symbols led to the identification in 1921 of the central image as the Sun God Tonatiuh. The Calendar Stone was then renamed the Stone of the Sun. In 1979, new research linked the glyph dates to ordinary dates. 13-Reed marked not just the beginning of the fifth world period, but also relates to C.E. 1427, and the beginnings of the Aztec empire under the new emperor Itzcoatl.

GROWING UP AZTEC

The **Codex** Mendoza was written after the Spanish conquest, in 1541. Its vivid paintings in the Aztec style are accompanied by Spanish descriptions that together give a very detailed picture of everyday Aztec life. It takes us on an intimate journey through Aztec schools, shows us the often difficult relationships between parents and children, and describes the sometimes strange and sometimes familiar tensions and joys of getting married.

Cherished children

For the Aztecs, the birth of a child was a time of joy and danger, both physically and spiritually. The baby was delivered by a professional midwife who cut the umbilical cord and prayed to Chalchiuhtlicue, the goddess of fertility and childbirth. If the baby was a boy, its umbilical cord was given to warriors to bury on a battlefield. If it was a girl, the cord was placed beneath the hearth in the parents' home, near the stone used for grinding corn.

◁ *This miniature mask represents the god Ixtiton. He brought children peaceful sleep.*

The Codex Mendoza describes how a newborn baby's name was chosen.

The parents consulted priests whose job it was to discover the supernatural influences associated with the time and date of the birth. If the date of birth was lucky, the baby was named the following day. If born on an unlucky day, a better naming date was chosen. The name itself was announced at dawn by the midwife who had delivered the baby.

A future life

Soon after birth, baby boys were given miniature symbols of their future adult life according to their father's occupation. Some had a warrior's shield, others a goldsmith's tool or a featherworker's knife. Baby girls were given a broom, a spindle full of cotton thread, or a basket. Once this had been done, young boys would run through the streets shouting the newborn's name and carrying a special meal of bean stew and parched corn. The Codex Mendoza reveals that boys and girls were welcomed equally into Aztec families, and were described in loving terms such as "precious necklaces" or "beautiful feathers."

◁ *These are miniature examples of an Aztec spear and spear thrower, which were given to Aztec boys.*

Archaeology Challenge

One particular profession for which we have **archaeological** evidence is that of the paper makers. Most codices were made from native paper produced from the inner bark of the fig tree. **Excavations** at Yautepec discovered the square ridged-stones that were used to beat strips of bark fiber into flat paper. These were then trimmed to the required size, and given a chalky-white varnish onto which a scribe would draw, and then paint his images. According to the Codex Mendoza, every year saw 24,000 reams of paper paid as tax to the Aztecs.

Life for children

Girls were educated at home and were usually married by age fifteen. Aztec boys entered school at age fifteen. If boys were commoners they attended the *telpochcalli,* where rules were strict. Teen boys learned how to build roads and repair temples, but they were mainly taught the skills of war. Military training was given by experienced warriors. Boys graduated from carrying equipment for others to using their own weapons in battle.

Noble children lived in more exclusive schools known as *calmecac. Calmecac* were associated with temples, and their aim was to educate the next generation of leaders in government, the priesthood, and the army. The *calmecac* were well stocked with **codices** that students used to learn about the gods, warfare, and **astronomical** events. Students were trained in religious matters, from sweeping temple floors to playing music for **rituals.** By the time boys left the *calmecac,* they had become full-trained warriors.

A boy's education before school
Education for Aztec boys before they entered school was based on teaching them life skills. These skills included fighting, but also using boats and canoes in order to work on the chinampas *(floating gardens).*

This farmer has punished his son, age twelve, by stripping him naked, tying him up, and throwing him into a muddy puddle in the street.

This farmer teaches his thirteen-year-old son how to carry loads and how to use a canoe.

Here, a farmer shows his fourteen-year-old son how to fish.

A boy of this age would be expected to earn his keep or face harsh punishments.

A girl's education before school

Education for girls before the age of fifteen took place at home. A girl would be taught skills that she would need to keep a home of her own.

▽ The illustrations in the Codex Mendoza about bringing up children use the following key to show age and food. The red dots represent the age of a child in years, while the yellow ovals illustrate the number of tortillas they were allowed to eat per day. This was an indication of the maturity of a child.

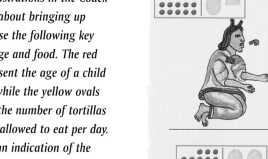

Once she reached the age of twelve, a daughter would be taught to grind corn and make tortillas. She would be expected to do this daily when she became a mother herself.

This thirteen-year-old girl is being taught how to sweep the floor by her mother. Aztecs believed that when they cleaned, they were helping the gods purify the world.

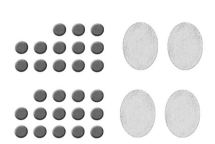

This mother is teaching her fourteen-year-old daughter how to use a backstrap loom to weave. One end is fastened to the wall, while the other is wrapped around her back. By moving backwards and forwards, she can tighten or loosen the threads.

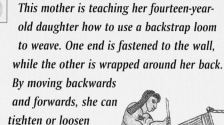

DID YOU KNOW? Punishments for bad behavior included being thrown into a hot fire.

35

School days and marriage

The **Codex** Mendoza states that young men were usually married by their early twenties, and young women by the age of fifteen. Parents and relatives selected a suitable bride for their son and employed an elderly woman as **matchmaker**. Discussions with the bride's family involved negotiations about the **dowry** paid to them by the groom's family. The marriage ceremony began with feasting in the bride's house during which guests were given food, *pulque* drink, tobacco, and flowers. The bride was then carried in a torch-lit procession to her husband's house, where she sat on a reed mat with her husband and they tied their robes together. Family advice followed and several days later a final feast saw the exchange of gifts between the two families.

▲ *This scene from the Codex Mendoza shows the training necessary to become a warrior. The more detailed the clothing, the higher the rank.*

Marriage and politics

An Aztec man could have more than one wife, though he had to be able to support them. Ordinary people could usually only afford one wife, but nobles often had more. King Nezahualpilli of the city of Texcoco was said to have had 2,000 wives and 144 children. In all marriages there could be only one head wife, and she controlled all secondary wives. Political marriages between the emperor and the ruling families of other cities were a way of making diplomatic alliances.

Married life

Although women had separate roles to men, they were not considered inferior. Men were away from home for much of the year, often fighting for the emperor, and the women were left behind to take care of the household. A man's role was to protect his wife and earn enough money to support his family. A woman was expected to be obedient to her husband. In the Codex Mendoza wives were told, "Obey your husband cheerfully. Do not scorn him for you will offend the goddess Xochiquetzal."

△ *This image from the Codex Mendoza shows Aztec wives cooking at home.*

Morals and divorce

The Codex Mendoza states that Aztec morals and behavior were strictly controlled and punishments were severe. Divorce was possible for men and women if a marriage failed. If a wife was unable to have children or neglected her duties, or if a husband beat his wife, divorce was granted by the courts. If a husband was at fault, his wife was free to remarry, keep **custody** of any children, and was granted half of everything the couple had owned.

▷ *A stone statue from the Great Temple shows an Aztec woman carrying her child and a water pot.*

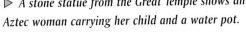

DID YOU KNOW? During a birth, an Aztec midwife shouted out battle cries to reflect the child fighting for life. **37**

WARFARE AND WARRIORS

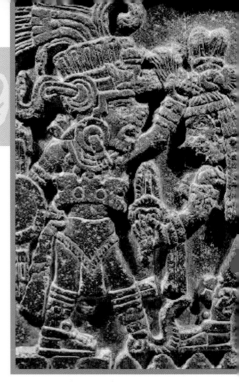

The Stone of Tizoc is a huge stone cylinder decorated with carvings of the emperor Tizoc at war. It was discovered buried near the cathedral in downtown Mexico City in December 1791. Together with the discovery of a temple outside Mexico City, statues of warriors, and evidence from the **codices**, archaeologists have been able to piece together Aztec beliefs about warfare.

The Stone of Tizoc

The Stone of Tizoc shows the emperor capturing the rulers of fifteen regions whose names are engraved in **glyphs** on

△ *A detail from the Stone of Tizoc shows the emperor holding the hair of an enemy.*

the Stone. Tizoc is shown grasping the hair of his enemies as a sign of his victory. The rays of the sun on the Stone's surface radiate out to the four directions of the empire, reflecting the spread of Tizoc's empire. The monument was **propaganda** because Tizoc was actually a failure as a general, and the victories celebrated here were in fact achieved before his reign began.

△ *Archaeologists think that this building in Malinalco was a ceremonial center for Eagle and Jaguar Knights.*

The Temple at Malinalco

High in the mountains southwest of Mexico City is the temple of Malinalco, dedicated to the two elite Aztec warrior societies of the Jaguar and the Eagle. This rock-cut **shrine** has an entrance carved in the shape of a giant serpent, and at the base of the stairway stand two stone jaguar statues. Inside there is a bench with a sculpted jaguar head and its paws flanked by two eagles, with a third eagle sculpture in the center of the floor. Archaeologists think the jaguar and eagle carvings were probably the ceremonial seats of the military governors of the region.

Eagle Knights

Archaeologists **excavating** at the Great Temple site in Mexico City found two life-size pottery statues guarding the entry to the main room. Each one represented a man dressed in the feathers of a giant eagle, with his head peering out of the bird's open beak. By comparing these statues with illustrations from the codices, archaeologists realized that they were looking at two Eagle Knights—one of the two great Aztec military societies.

Jaguar Knights

The Codex Nuttall describes and illustrates the clothing, weapons, and tactics of warriors. Jaguar Knights are shown wearing large jaguar-head helmets, carrying their javelins, spearthrowers, and shields. This image is also shown in the Codex Borbonicus, where warriors are shown dressed as jaguars, walking into battle. The Codex Mendoza shows several burning temples, the Aztec glyph for military conquest, and large Aztec warriors grasping the hair of smaller, defeated enemies.

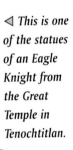

◁ *This is one of the statues of an Eagle Knight from the Great Temple in Tenochtitlan.*

DID YOU KNOW? One of the reasons for going to war was to capture victims for sacrifice. **39**

Ancient Mexican war

Ways of war

The Mexican way of war was different from that practiced by Europeans. The Aztecs and their neighbors waged war to impose taxes on their enemies, and to capture prisoners for sacrifice to the gods. The key to success, as the **Codex** Mendoza illustrates, was fabulous wealth in endless lists of tribute (taxes) paid by defeated enemies, not dead bodies. A ceremonial wooden war drum from the mountain temple of Malinalco shows how much **ritual** there was in Mexican warfare. Many warriors dressed in elaborate, colorful, and impractical clothing and headdresses. For Aztec warriors who did die in battle, their souls became butterflies and hummingbirds.

Archaeology Challenge

Archaeologists think that there might be a similar temple to that of the Jaguar Knights on the south side of the Great Temple that remains unexcavated. This is because the Aztecs created a world where everything was in balance. Also, Jaguar and Eagle Knights played an equal role in warfare and sacrifice at the Great Temple.

Weapons

Aztec warriors wore body armor of quilted cotton, colorful clothing, and headdresses. Shields decorated with feathers, mosaic or gold, and turquoise inlay have also been found by archaeologists, as well as weapons including the javelin, bow, sling, and sword. The obsidian-tipped javelin was launched with a spear-thrower, which added force and distance to the weapon. The Aztec sword was a long shaft of wood whose edges were inset with blades sharp enough to **decapitate** a Spaniard's horse.

A warlike society

The Codex Mendoza describes how from the age of fifteen, boys were trained as warriors and dedicated themselves to Tezcatlipoca, the master of a warrior's fate. The Codex Magliabecchiano shows a **ball court** decorated with a human skull, indicating that even public games could end in death. Public monuments such as the Stone of the Warriors, found in Mexico City in 1897, also cast light on Aztec warfare. The Stone shows the emperor Ahuitzotl and thirteen of his generals celebrating a military victory.

The War of Flowers

The War of Flowers, or **xochiyaotl,** was a special type of warfare. Its name refers to the colorful clothing of warriors, and how they fell in battle like a shower of blossoms. The Codex Chimalpopoca recorded flowery wars between the Aztecs and the Chalca people. In the *Book of the Gods and Rites,* Spanish priest Diego Durán describes flowery wars as designed especially to capture prisoners for sacrifice to the gods, rather than for conquest. Priests observed these battles and once they decided enough prisoners had been taken, the wars ended.

◁ *This scene from the Codex Chimalpopoca shows an Aztec War of Flowers.*

WHO WAS Montezuma I?

Montezuma I (ruled 1440–1469) was one of the longest-lived Aztec emperors. During his rule he led the army to many victories, expanding Aztec power and forcing many cities to pay him tribute, or taxes. But things did not always go well for the people under his rule. Between 1450–1452 a terrible drought caused many people to starve. The emperor did his best to feed them from grain stored in government warehouses.

DID YOU KNOW? Each *calpulli* sent a regiment of men to fight in the army.

41

AZTEC ARCHAEOLOGY TODAY

The investigations at the Great Temple in Mexico City were more than **archaeological excavations**. They also represented a source of pride for modern Mexicans who wish to celebrate their Aztec past as well as their Spanish heritage. Modern archaeology embraces such ideas, mixing cultural traditions with history and science to present a dazzling past to younger generations.

The Shrine of Guadeloupe

Mexican society today is a mix of Catholic religion and the old Aztec ways. An example of the old ways is the **Christian** cult of the Virgin of Guadeloupe at Tepeyac in northern Mexico City. Originally this area was sacred to the Aztec goddess Tonantzin who was addressed in prayers as "Our Mother." After the Spanish conquest, the area became Christian when a shepherd who had converted to Christianity had a vision ofthe Virgin Mary and built a church on that spot to honor her.

△ *Men dressed as jaguars re-enact a blood sacrifice to the Jaguar God.*

Blood for the Jaguar God

The remote mountain village of Acatlán in southwest Mexico was founded during Aztec times. Each spring, people hold a **ritual** which echoes blood sacrifices by the Aztec Jaguar Knights. Young men dressed in jaguar costumes fight each other in pairs on the **summit** of a local mountain known as Blue Mountain. The fights begin in early May, and villagers believe that if they shed the powerful blood of young men, the Jaguar God will be pleased and send rain to fertilize the corn crop.

Day of the Dead

Another example of the mixing of the old and new is the Day of the Dead, or All Saints Day, celebrations that take place every year in early November. Before the Spanish conquest, skulls and skeletons were featured in Aztec art in part to frighten and intimidate their enemies. Today, miniatures skulls and skeletons are made of sugar and chocolate as candy for children. Families spend the night at the graves of their relatives that they adorn with brightly colored flowers. As did the Aztecs, many modern Mexicans believe that if you do not honor the dead in this way they return to haunt you.

◁ Mexico's highest mountain, Pico de Orizaba, is the site of an Aztec shrine found in 2001.

New finds

In 2001, a stone Aztec **shrine** dating from the 1400s was found some 13,976 feet (4,260 meters) up the 17,979 foot- (5,480 meter-) high Pico de Orizaba, Mexico's highest mountain. It may have been built to honor the rain god Tlaloc. It is in a line with two nearby peaks, La Malinche and Cerro Tlaloc, suggesting it was also used by the Aztecs to watch the stars.

Archaeology Challenge

For information about the details of daily life in ancient times, archaeologists often rely on middens—ancient garbage dumps. By searching through the household waste of past times, they can learn a surprising amount about how people lived, the work they did around the house, the food they ate, and the vessels they prepared it in. The study of some Aztec middens has unearthed not only thousands of fragments of broken cooking pots and storage jars, but also many tiny clay figurines, thought to have been used in household religious rituals.

TIMELINE OF THE AZTEC EMPIRE

For the early part of their history, the Aztecs were a nomadic tribe that wandered up and down the Valley of Mexico, seeking land in which to settle. In 1325, they finally found an island on Lake Texcoco. By 1350 they had built Tenochtitlan, which was to become the center of their empire. The Aztec civilization lasted just over 200 years before the Spaniards took their country from them in 1521.

C.E.

About 1100–1200
The Aztecs leave their original home in the wilds of northern Mexico in search of a better home with more land.

About 1300
The Aztecs arrive in the Valley of Mexico as a small, hungry band of homeless wanderers.

1325
The Aztecs settle on a small island near the shore of Lake Texcoco, where they will build their future capital, Tenochtitlan.

About 1350
By this time, the Aztecs are one of about twenty different tribes all struggling for power in the Valley of Mexico.

1376
Acamapichtli, a member of the ruling family of the neighboring city-state of Culhuacan, becomes Aztec ruler. He is the first Aztec leader whose name is still known today.

1426
The Aztec ruler Chimalpopoca is killed on the orders of the king of the powerful neighboring city-state of Azcapotzalco.

1427
The new Aztec king, Itzcoatl, makes a Triple Alliance with two other nearby city-states to take revenge on Azcapotzalco.

1428
The Aztecs and their allies conquer Azcapotzalco, destroying the city. They then become the chief powers in the Valley of Mexico.

1440
Montezuma I, the greatest Aztec emperor, comes to the throne.

1450–1452
A terrible drought strikes the Aztec lands, leaving thousands of people dead.

1473
The Aztecs conquer the neighboring island of Tlatelolco in Lake Texcoco, and join it by a causeway to their capital of Tenochtitlan. The capital's main marketplace will develop there.

1487
The Great Temple in Tenochtitlan is rebuilt bigger than ever. More than 20,000 human victims are sacrificed in a four-day ceremony when it is completed.

1502–1520
Montezuma II becomes the last Aztec emperor.

1519
Spanish **conquistadors** led by Hernán Cortés arrive on the coast of Mexico.

1520
Montezuma II invites Cortés and his soldiers to stay as guests in his palace. They respond by taking him prisoner. He is finally killed by his own people when he makes a speech telling them not to resist the Spaniards, who are then driven out of the city.

1521
Cortés returns with more troops and besieges the city. It falls after a 93-day battle. The Spaniards enter in triumph and take control of the whole Aztec empire.

1535
Mexico becomes a colony of Spain.

1547
Hernán Cortés dies in Spain.

1567
Cortés' body is brought back to Mexico and is buried in the cathedral built using the stones from the Aztec's Great Temple.

TIMELINE OF AZTEC ARCHAEOLOGY

1520s
Spanish conquistador Hernán Cortés writes several letters to the King of Spain about his experiences in Aztec Mexico.

1540s
Spanish viceroy Antonio de Mendoza commissions the **Codex** Mendoza to depict Aztec culture for the King of Spain.

Friar Bernardino de Sahagún compiles a book titled the *Florentine Codex: General History of the Things of New Spain* on Aztec history, customs, and religion.

1570s
Spanish conquistador Bernal Díaz del Castillo's account of what he had witnessed during the conquest, *The True History of the Conquest of New Spain,* is published in Spain.

1790
Workers building drains in the center of Mexico City discover a huge statue of the Aztec goddess Coatlicue. The statue is later reburied because Spanish priests consider it "devilish."

1791
Workers employed on the same job make two other important discoveries, both carved circular stones weighing many tons. One will become known as the Calendar Stone, the other as the Stone of Tizoc.

1821
Mexico wins independence from Spain, making it easier for foreign archaeologists to visit the country.

1823
The statue of Coatlicue is dug up again and put in a museum.

1884
Mexican archaeologist Leopoldo Batres starts to **excavate** the ancient city of Teotihuacan, which flourished in the Valley of Mexico 1,000 years before the Aztecs arrived.

1900
Further Aztec finds are made when new sewers are laid in Mexico City.

1964
The National Museum of Anthropology opens in Mexico City to house the world's best collection of Aztec treasures.

1966
Construction of a new underground railway system begins in Mexico City. Many Aztec **artifacts** are discovered.

1967
The temple of Ehecatl-Quetzalcoatl is discovered when the Pino Suarez subway station is built.

1978
Workers laying electrical cables in the center of Mexico City discover the Stone of Coyolxauhqui, another important Aztec artifact.

1978–1982
Following the worker's find, a major **archaeological** project gets under way to **excavate** the remains of the Aztec Great Temple and surrounding buildings.

1988
The Stone of Montezuma I is unearthed from the gardens of the Archbishop's Palace in Mexico City.

1992
More than 200 precious metal bars are recovered from a shipwreck off Grand Bahama in the West Indies. The bars are thought to be Aztec gold, silver, and copper plundered by the Spaniards and melted down. Archaeologists date the bars to between 1521–1535—around the time when the Aztec empire collapsed.

2001
Archaeologists discover a stone Aztec **shrine** on the Pico de Orizaba mountain in Mexico. Built to honor the rain god Tlaloc, it dates from the 1400s.

2002
Remains of Aztec city are found under the 18th century Chapultepec castle by archaeologists. This is the first time parts of the city have been found in the suburbs of modern Mexico City. Archaeologists discovered fragments of ceramics, figurines of gods, and bones needles used for needlework.

GLOSSARY

ancestor

person from whom someone is descended

aqueduct

pipe or channel designed to carry water

archaeology

scientific excavation and study of the remains of past societies, such as buildings, artwork, dead bodies, tools, pottery, and other objects

artifact

object made by people, such as a tool or an ornament. Archaeologists often use the word "artifacts" to describe the objects they find that were made by people in past times.

astronomy

scientific study of the stars, planets, and other space bodies that make up the universe

ball court

area of ground on which a ball game is played

bias

leaning toward a particular viewpoint

calmecac

school for the children of nobles

Christian

person who follows the Christian religion, believing Jesus Christ is the son of God

chronicle

register of events, often in the order in which they happened

codex (plural: codices)

book or books filled with a picture-based language called pictographs

conquistador

Spanish word for "conqueror," describing the Spanish soldiers who conquered much of Central and South America in the 1500s

currency

type of money particular to a country

custody

care for or guard someone

decapitate

slice the head off something

dismember

cut into pieces

dowry

property or money given to a bride by a groom's family

excavate

dig up a building or area of land in order to look for ancient objects, ruins, or other evidence of the past

flint

hard stone flaked to form a primitive tool or weapon

friar

member of certain special orders of Christian monks who go out to preach their message in public

glyph

carved character or symbol

imperial

something characteristic of an empire

jade

precious green stone, used to make jewelry and statues

macehualtin

name of an Aztec commoner

matchmaker

person paid to arrange a marriage

mayeques

landless but free peasants

missionary

person who tries to convert another person to their religion

Mixtec

culture of southern Mexico that existed just before the Aztecs

monk

person belonging to one of the various Christian religious orders.

mythology

collection of stories associated with a particular culture

Nahuatl

official language of the Aztecs. It is still spoken today.

New World

North and South America

pagan

person or thing not identified with any of the main religions

pictograph

writing that uses pictures rather than letters; so, a picture of a house means "house"

pochteca

name given to Aztec merchants who had special rights and privileges in society.

prejudice

opinion formed without examination of the facts

propaganda

material spread to support a cause

ritual

special words and actions of a religious service or ceremony

sculpture

work a material such as stone into a three-dimensional figure

shrine

sacred place, usually where people worship the body or statue of a god, saint, or other holy person. For the Aztecs, a small building sacred to a god, often set on top of a stepped pyramid.

siege

surround and blockade a city in an attempt to capture it

skull rack

rack to display the skulls of sacrifice victims

stingray

poisonous fish

summit

highest point of something

telpochcalli

school for Aztec commoners

tlachtli

game played in Central America in which players tried to knock a rubber ball through hoops without using their feet or hands

tlacotin

Aztec name for a slave

tortilla

thin Mexican cake or bread

xochiyaotl

Aztec name for a special type of war called the War of Flowers. Warriors fought to show their skill and take captives for sacrifice, rather than killing each other.

FURTHER READING

Chrisp, Peter. *The Aztecs*. Chicago: Raintree, 2000.

Dawson, Imogene. *Clothes and Crafts in Aztec Times*. Milwaukee: Gareth Stevens, 2000.

Hall, Eleanor. *Life Among the Aztec*. Farmington Hills, Mich.: Gale Group, 2004.

Hull, Robert. *The Aztecs*. Chicago: Raintree, 1998.

MacDonald, Fiona. *You Wouldn't Want to be an Aztec Sacrifice: Gruesome Things You'd Rather Not Know*. Danbury, Conn.: Franklin Watts, 2001.

Morgan, Nina. *The Aztecs*. Chicago: Raintree, 1998.

Rees, Rosemary. *The Aztecs*. Chicago: Heinemann Library, 1999.

Steele, Philip. *The Aztec News*. Milwaukee: Gareth Stevens, 2001.

Wyborny, Sheila. *Life During the Aztec Empire*. Farmington Hills, Mich.: Blackbirch Press, 2003.

INDEX